tennis for everyone

tennis for everyone

WITH OFFICIAL USLTA RULES

PAULINE BETZ ADDIE

 Published by **Acropolis Books Ltd.,** Washington, D.C. 20009

Other books by Pauline Betz Addie:

Wings on My Tennis Shoes
Tennis for Teenagers

ACROPOLIS BOOKS LTD.

Colortone Building, 2400 17th St., N.W.
Washington, D.C. 20009

Printed in the United States of America by
COLORTONE PRESS Creative Graphics Inc., *Washington, D.C. 20009*

Library of Congress Catalog Number 72-12392
International Standard Book Number
(Cloth) 0-87491-149-4
(Paper) 0-87491-150-8

We gratefully acknowledge
the cooperation of the
United States
Lawn Tennis Association
in approving our use of
the official USLTA rules
in this tennis manual.

Our thanks
also to
Dick Darcey
for many
of the pictures in
Tennis For Everyone.

contents

introduction

The fastest growing indoor sport hardly is what you think—and there is no question about its outdoor popularity. Of course, the sport is tennis and the proliferation of what once was confined to the ladies and gentlemen on a lawny Sunday afternoon has been phenomenal.

Tennis is played on the playgrounds, on city streets, on clay, cement, grass and synthetic turf. It is a game for the child, the young adult, the weekender, the stay-in-shaper, the senior.

Tennis is everywhere. It's not only Wimbledon and Forest Hills and Newport and Cannes. It is a viable, exciting, fascinating sport, pasttime, recreation, hobby and status symbol. It is all of those and more.

What is the mystique of the game and is there a mystique? It's like everything else. Some can play well and some can't. Some people are more dedicated than others and will become champions—but only if they pay the price. Like freedom, championship ability is a hard-bought thing.

But there is a beginning in tennis. There is a way to learn it. You pick out your own slot. Do you want to play tournament tennis? Only you can judge—after you have played tournament tennis because there are competitions on every level.

Do you want to be good enough to feel that you're not embarrassing yourself when you take the court? That takes work, too. There is no easy way through the "boot camp" of tennis—the labyrinthine way before you emerge from the maze of instruction with some idea of your personal coordination and your necessary adjustments.

A cliche gets that way because there must be a nugget of eternal truth. For instance: one must crawl before walking—and a journey of a thousand miles begins with the first step. So be it.

Tennis is grace and form and stamina and coordination and athletic ability. It's a sport, of course, but it's also a form of a dance—the most intricate dance you have ever done.

Watch those feet. Move, move. Hit the ball. Balance, remember, balance. Position with balance. Anticipation with balance and position and on and on. After the awkward stage comes the grace, the know-how, the application of the lessons.

There are other compensations. Maybe mini-skirts have taken some of the glamor out of tennis shorts and brief skirts for girls—but have they? Tennis liberated women long before it became a cause and a crusade. The Twentieth Century girl long ago adopted shorts on the tennis court, stopped hiding in broom closets when somebody looked at her ankles, abandoned riding side-saddle to the hounds and liberated herself. The tennis racquet has been mightier than the lectern and the soap box.

The world is made of participants and peepers. Too many people are content to watch sports—to peep and not participate. There is room for both. I am not against watching an exciting sports event on TV. But there is no substitute for a participant sport. Certainly, tennis is one of the best of these—a game one can play from the cradle of youth to the rocking chair of seniority.

This book, then, is designed for anyone who wants to learn to play tennis. Its aim is to show you the basic shots and to talk about the frustrations and joys of mastering them. It is geared to the needs of the average player, the person who wants to play a good, passable game of tennis. Perhaps some of you younger players may make it all the way to the top. That would be an extra dividend. But, in the main, I hope to instill in my own pupils and readers of this book the thought that tennis is a game of fun and pleasure and that it has few peers as a life-long social game.

Tennis is much like golf in that the big man (or woman) is not always the best. The game is designed for those with grace, speed and stamina. Perhaps in some sports a good big man always will beat a good little man but there are many ways in tennis to overcome disadvantages in size and sex. There is no reason why any healthy young person (or even some of the healthy, older ones) can't play a good game of tennis. The better you play, the more fun the game becomes. And at any stage, it's far more stimulating than jogging.

In the chapters that follow, I will show you the various basic shots and some of the more exotic ones that can't be learned over the course of the summer. But, remember, there's a catch to instant tennis, too. You must practice to perfect any of these shots. However, even if your shots are not perfect, you won't be barred from the courts. Quite acceptable tennis can be played, especially in doubles, with a limited bag of shots and a certain amount of beguiling chatter (sometimes called "gamesmanship" or "con" to hide your inadequacies).

Tennis is a social sport. It has been played for centuries although the type of tennis, "lawn tennis," with which this book deals, actually dates only from 1874 when Major Walter Wingfield patented what he called "a new and improved portable court for playing the ancient game of tennis."

The first U.S. championship was held in Newport, R.I., in August, 1876, and I suppose the origin of the Newport environment did much to add the social flavor to tennis that it still enjoys. The Men's Davis Cup competition among the nations of the world for the great silver cup, plus the Women's Wightman Cup and Federation Cup matches, have added to the international prestige of this great game and the many tournaments for juniors and older, sponsored by the United States Lawn Tennis Association and the various tennis clubs in every neighborhood, have given the game its widespread popularity.

Tennis was given a tremendous shot in the arm in 1968 when "open tennis" finally was approved. Pros and amateurs were merged, prize money rivaled that earned by name golfers, television coverage increased dramatically (and financially), and it seemed that the entire world suddenly had become tennis conscious.

Perhaps that is why most of us are familiar with the great names of today's tennis world—Rod Laver, Ken Rosewall, Ilie Nastase, Arthur Ashe, John Newcombe, Stan Smith and then those Virginia Slims Ladies—Billie Jean King, Rosie Casals, Nancy Richey Gunter, Evonne Goolagong, and the newest young star—Chris Evert

You may not aspire to their heights and your ambition may be only to be tolerated as a partner or opponent by your average playing husband but tennis can be a sport which will stay with you and which you can enjoy all your life.

All sorts of athletes and celebrities play tennis. Ted Williams knew something about hitting a moving ball. He was one of the greatest hitters of all time. He took up tennis after he had retired and for all his genius in hitting a moving ball he confessed that tennis threw him —but at the beginning only. If you know Williams, you know that nothing (except the Texas Rangers) ever threw him for long.

Curiously, another baseball Hall of Famer, Hank Greenberg, is an avowed tennis addict. Greenberg, now a wealthy investment banker, plays whenever and wherever he can. He has developed into a formidable player, too, employing some of the dedication and physical skill that made him a great baseball figure.

The movie colony has its share of players who keep the courts busy at the Racket Club in Palm Springs and you're really not with it in Beverly Hills and Bel Aire if you don't have a tennis court or courts. Various celebrity tournaments have as contestants such entertainment figures as James Franciscus, Gary Crosby, Don Adams, Dick Crenna, Burt Bachrach, Steve Allen, Ed Ames, Cornel Wilde, Clint Eastwood, Dean Martin, Charleton Heston, Dan Rowan and Lloyd Bridges.

On the political front, such personalities as Spiro Agnew, Sargent Shriver, and Senators George McGovern, Charles Percy and Jacob Javits are "steady" players—meaning they always make room at least once a week for a game of tennis.

The game needs no endorsement. Everybody is playing tennis now. Why not learn how to play it well—right from the start; right at YOUR age?

CHAPTER I
Forehand

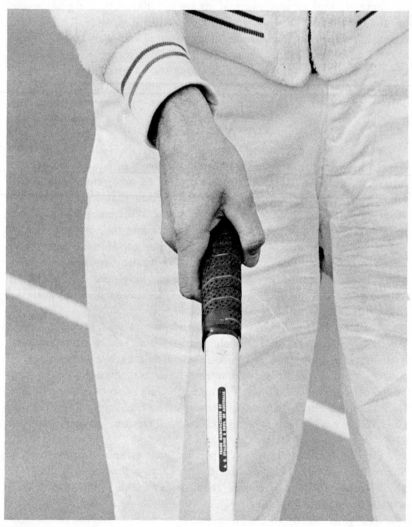

The forehand grip

Most professionals start a pupil by teaching him the forehand. Trying to learn the backhand is so discouraging that the second lesson will probably be from the golf professional.

Any shot which you hit on the right hand side of your body (left handers, of course, reverse all directions) is called a forehand. Now there are many queer looking shots which still qualify as the forehand but you should try to learn something resembling an orthodox stroke. You swing at the side something like the batter in baseball; your body pivot is similar to the golfer; and your feet shuffle about like a basketball player. All of your previous sports, including dancing, will help you and yet, tennis is a distinct sport which should be learned correctly. The athlete without lessons, unless he is a good mimic who has watched much tennis, invariably hits the ball with a sort of overhead push rather than the classic forehand swing. Much later in life he will wail "why didn't I learn to play the right way?"

The Eastern "shake hands" grip is used by a majority of players. Place the palm of your hand flat on the strings of the racket and slide it down to the end of the handle with the fingers slightly apart. Then consult your pro to make sure that you've arrived at the proper grip. Of course there have been some fine forehands with different grips and if you have for years been putting the ball away with a big Western forehand, don't change to be with the majority. And what better forehand has existed than the two-fisted bomb of Pancho Segura? Fred Perry, the great English champion, used the Continental grip and had a fine shot with a maximum of wrist action. However, if you're a beginner I would certainly advise starting with the grip which most players believe proves the easiest method to hit all types of shots, the Eastern.

THE FOREHAND SWING

It is not too difficult to learn the forehand swing. The problems arise when you're forced not only to swing correctly but also to judge the bounce of the ball and to time your swing to contact the ball at the right place. Even in golf when you are hitting a stationary ball, somehow the practice swings are beautiful but everything goes up in smoke when the ball appears. (Arnold Palmer may not have that problem but I do!)

Try swinging a few times before adding the ball to the picture. Stand with your left side to the net and start the racket head back as you shift your weight back to your right foot. I believe that, at least in

Weight and racket are both back at the start of the forehand.

Contact is just ahead of the left toe and at arm's length. Weight has shifted to the front foot.

Hips and shoulders are now square with the net.

I would rather see the finish with the elbow a bit straighter, but Nancy Ornstein hits a wicked forehand.

17

the beginning stages, the backswing should find the racket slightly below waist high, past the right side with a bend in the elbow. This puts you in the same position as if you were going to slap and follow through with the palm of your hand. If you can find someone who doesn't mind being slapped, go through the slapping motion and you'll find your weight shifting naturally to your left side. Presuming that you are going to contact the ball about waist high, the racket head should start fairly low and come up through the ball at impact. Your wrist should be firm but not locked and your elbow should straighten out as you contact the ball.

Pivot your hips and shoulders a la baseball as you move through the ball. While it is true that the good players have quite a swing flourish and lengthy follow-through, start out by holding the finish at a point approximately opposite your left shoulder (point towards left corner of court), with racket face flat—i. e. strings straight up and down. Another way to get the feel of the entire swing is to take your practice swing and release the racket as you follow through. (You should have two rackets and a clear space for throwing when using this method.)

HITTING THE BALL ON THE MOVE

Before attempting to hit the ball on the run, learn to bounce it for yourself and hit it over the net. In order to make sure that my pupils hit the ball in front of the left toe, I make them stand behind the baseline and throw the ball up out of the left hand so that it will bounce in front of the line. It is actually quite difficult to toss the ball to the right spot. Almost every beginner, whether bouncing the ball for himself or trying to hit one which has been hit over the net to him, makes the mistake of hitting the ball too close to the body. You hear the clunk of the wood or the swish of the racket as it comes up empty. You have to exaggerate your distance from the ball in order to learn what a big reach you have with that racket.

Besides learning the swing and judging the ball, you must have the correct timing. Boys for the most part are more athletic than girls and they've been playing catch since about their year one. They seem to have instinctive timing and it doesn't take most of them very long to start hitting the tennis ball. But I can remember starting my daughter at about age eight (my four boys began at six) and having her watch the ball go by, saying "But, you didn't tell me when to swing." For those who don't know "when to swing," I have a little chant to help

Avid tennis player Vice President Spiro Agnew still going strong after a long match has worn down his younger opponents.

them time the ball. As you toss the ball up out of your left hand say "up," as you shift your weight and racket back, say "back" and as the ball bounces up about waist high and you shift your weight and racket forward, say "swing."

Once you can bounce the ball for yourself and hit it over the net, you're ready to have a parent or a self-sacrificing friend stand at the net and toss you some balls to hit. If you try playing with some one of your own ability (or lack of it) you'll spend most of your time walking to the fence behind you to pick up the balls you've missed. Neither of you will be able to place the ball where the other one has a chance of reaching it. Within about 10 minutes you'll conclude that tennis is no fun at all and find something interesting to do. Search for a player better than you are. You must learn to hit the easy well-placed shots first in order to groove a swing. Gradually you can progress to the more difficult shots as your timing and judgment improve. It will take hitting thousands and thousands of balls for you to acquire a decent forehand and yet it won't take too long for you to start having the thrill of hitting some of them back over the net.

Everyone working on a shot needs a good player who can place the ball at a spot where it is easy to hit. I had one pupil who was desperately trying to improve her backhand and I advised her to have her husband stand at the net and hit hundreds of easy balls to her backhand. She replied that it would be far easier for her to get **my** husband to hit them to her and it's undoubtedly true that most husbands don't feel that love, honor and cherish includes hitting balls to the backhand.

It seems easier for a pupil to time and judge the ball when I stand at the net than when I am hitting to him from the backcourt but eventually (say by the second lesson) I rouse him from his dream world where the ball is always placed at the right spot and make him start moving. Meanwhile, I've kept on with my "up," "back," "swing" chant; the "up" as I've hit the ball, the "back" with the pupil's racket and weight starting back as the ball leaves my racket, and the "swing" as he steps forward and contacts the ball. This seems to impart a certain rhythm and balance and gives a smooth rather than a jerky swing. When returning balls, wait in the "ready position." Face the net and cradle the throat of the racket in your left hand.

Ready position . . . !

FOOTWORK

Footwork is most important and this too can be first practiced without the complicating presence of the ball. Let's suppose that the ball is only a step or two away from you. Start with the right foot and never shift your weight to the left. Simply drag the left foot up to the right and then start on the right again. Whether you have to move sideways, backwards, or towards the net, you'll be using that same shuffle movement so that you'll always be in a position to move your weight into the ball. As you approach the ball, the last step with your right foot will be a pivot so that your hips and shoulders also will turn and you will be completely sideways as you start your swing. Your racket should start back as you start after the ball so that by the time you reach the ball, the racket head is back in position. Stand on the baseline and work on this all across the court and pretty soon you'll get the idea and won't feel that you're practicing to be crippled. Naturally, if you have a lot of court to cover, you'll pick up both feet as if you were running the 100 yard dash but as you reach the ball your footwork should again be the pivot of your weight onto the right side. The step to the left foot should be made towards the net (although usually the stance will be slightly closed—the left foot a bit forward of the right) as a step across towards the side fence almost locks the body and makes it difficult to pivot. Basketball is good training for tennis footwork as a player has to be moving quickly in all directions.

But the best way to practice tennis is simply to hit tennis balls. A backboard is excellent practice as it is not going to miss (although you may miss the backboard). Dick Dell of Bethesda, Maryland, now a ranking player, lived next to the Edgemoor Club and when four years old would spend hours on the backboard. Now there's an incentive for any harried mother to try to interest the young fry in tennis.

PLACING THE BALL

Jean Hoxie, the fine teacher who operated a tennis camp in Hamtramck, Michigan, has had marked success with her pupils by stressing consistency and accuracy through aiming at objects on the court and also dividing the backboard into certain areas where a player must place hundreds of balls.

I feel that I really learned to play tennis through hitting against our garage door. The door wasn't available after school since my brother picked that time to practice basketball on the driveway and he was bigger than I was. However, at six in the morning the area was free and I'd pound away until school time. I don't know that the neighbors appreciated it but already we weren't too popular on either side since our police dog had dug up everyone's freshly planted gardens and our baseballs or basketballs or footballs were forever going through unopened windows. Fortunately we moved rather often and were always in a position to antagonize new neighbors.

At first you will be so concerned with merely getting the ball back that "who aims?" will be your reaction to anyone's suggestion that you hit it to a certain place. A popular misconception is that you point your rackethead towards the spot where you would like the ball to go. But actually the point of contact determines whether you are going to place the ball crosscourt or down the line. Test this out by bouncing a ball close to your right foot and following through way around to the left. Unless you've done something very strange the ball should go to your right because at the moment of contact the face of the racket was pointed in that direction. Now bounce a ball well in front of your left foot and use the same swing and follow through. If the ball doesn't go to your left, or cross court, write and tell me.

One common difficulty when you are playing is to realize that the ball will not bounce up in the place where it hits. Instead of charging into the ball at full force and having it hit you in the stomach, stop well behind the bounce and you will find the ball coming back to you. The pros are able to hit the ball on the rise but it will be better and easier for you to let the ball settle down to a waist high position.

When you have an acceptable flat forehand, you can start to learn variations of it such as chop and topspin. Initially, just learn the simple flat forehand with a large margin of safety—clear the net by a few feet and try to hit the ball fairly deep in the court but not too near the lines. Don't try to slug the ball like Pancho Gonzales until the second year.

FOREHAND SUMMARY AND TESTS

Mistakes to watch for—Have your professional check your problems

1. Too short a backswing
2. Not reaching enough for ball
3. Too open a stance
4. Bad follow through
5. Does not stay back of bounce of the ball
6. Racket face too open—would you believe—too closed?
7. Wrist not firm
8. Contacts ball too late, too early
9. Bad grip
10. Apparently has eyes closed

PRO'S SUGGESTIONS

11.
12.
13.
14.
15.

In order to learn to control the ball you might have your teacher give you a few tests.

Test 1. Take 25 balls (if you can find them) and see how many you can bounce for yourself and hit over the net. **Test 2.** Then have the pro stand just across the net and place 25 balls on the forehand side for you. **Test 3.** Next have him move to the back court and hit you 25 shots placed fairly close to you. **Test 4.** Let him hit the ball a bit harder on the next 25 and make you move for them. **Test 5.** And last, try to return 25 medium paced serves with your fast improving forehand.

SCORES

Test 1.   Number in ————

Test 2.   ————

Test 3.   ————

Test 4.   ————

Test 5.   ————

Rod Laver reaches for a wide forehand.

CHAPTER II
Backhand

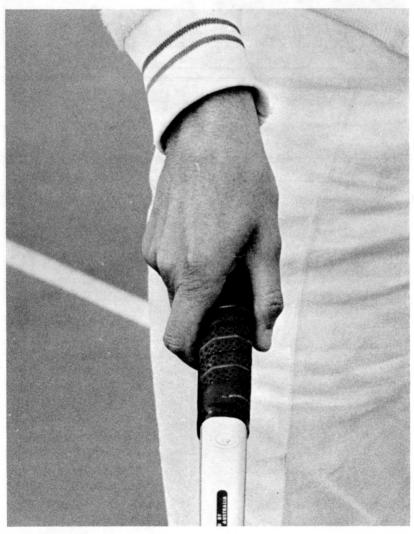

The backhand grip.

My sister and I started tennis at the same time and our practice sessions were usually abruptly terminated when one of us would run crying to mother with the complaint that "she hit it to my backhand." Who could be expected to rally (especially with a sister) unless the ball was placed to the forehand? Unfortunately I proved to be fast enough to run around the backhand and for years it was to be relatively impotent compared with the forehand. But as the competition improved I found my backhand under constant attack and finally began to work hard to develop it.

The first essential is the proper grip. Holding the Eastern forehand, move your hand approximately a quarter turn to the left and place the thumb diagonally along the handle of the racket. The thumb position may vary but virtually all of the good amateurs and professionals, with the exception of Andres Gimeno, turn the hand so that it is in the same position as for a Continental forehand. The wrist should be firm. As on the forehand, have the professional check your grip.

UNORTHODOX GRIPS

Many players have unorthodox methods of holding the racket while hitting a tennis ball.

Oddly, many of the junior players of today start and continue with a two-handed backhand. It could be because of the popularity of the "switch-hitter" in baseball or perhaps it is because the starting age is getting younger and younger and the six and seven year olds find two hands a necessity. Chris Evert has a beautiful two handed backhand and her younger sister Jeanne uses the same fluent two handed stroke. Davis Cupper Harold Solomon of Maryland also has a big two handed backhand as do the new young stars Jim Connors and Billy Martin. Frew McMillen of South Africa hits everything except his serve with both hands while the only other two handed forehands belong to Pancho Segura and Rusty Addie.

The French word for backhand is "revers" and that is an apt description of the stroke. Each motion is exactly the opposite to your forehand.

The backhand is far from a natural motion. A right-handed person is used to moving to the right, to sweeping the floor on the right side (if you can't find anybody else to do it), or hitting a baseball right-handed. I always compare the backhand to a left-handed baseball swing so if you're a switch hitter you have a head start. Just keep in mind that you don't have to hit it over the fence à la Ted Williams, merely over the net.

If you can locate the fellow who let you slap his hand for your forehand practice, tell him your backhand is softer and may you please again borrow his hand. I feel that if you can reach the right position on the backswing a backhand is not too difficult. It is very similar to your position when you slap with the back of the hand. Don't use a racket but stand with your right side to the net and take your hand back as if you were going to slap. Your elbow will be bent and close to the body and you will find that you have automatically shifted your weight to the back foot and turned your right shoulder and hips away so that part of your back is towards the net. Now step forward on your right foot as you slap your friend's (?) hand and follow through. Let your shoulders and hips pivot so that the end of the swing finds you completely faced to the net, left toe still retaining contact with the ground.

Think of the racket as an extension of your arm and try a few practice swings with the same body action. You might try throwing the racket a few times to get the same feeling of release you'll need when actually hitting the ball. Sooner or later you'll have to stop practicing phantom picture swings and see what changes occur when the ball enters the picture.

THE STROKE

Bouncing the ball for yourself, to hit practice backhands, sometimes proves more difficult for a pupil than returning a well-placed easy shot from the other side of the net. You can use the same "up," "back" and "swing" timing device as for the forehand but the trouble stems from vain attempts to toss the ball to the proper spot. You should contact the ball slightly ahead of the right toe. I find that the easiest way to bounce the ball and to get your racket back into position is to stand with your right side towards the net and cross the left arm under the right. Toss the ball on "up," start the racket and weight back as you say "back" and the ball will have bounced and be ready for you about waist high as you let your weight and racket shift forward on "swing." Step towards the net with your right foot rather than in the direction of the side fence as, just as for the forehand, you don't want to lock yourself by stepping in one direction to swing or throw in

Chris Evert uses her two-handed backhand in Wightman Cup match at Wimbledon.

Everyone said that Silver Spring, Md., product Harold Solomon would never get anywhere with his unorthodox Western forehand and two-handed backhand . . .

. . . but he's just kept on winning!

The author, Pauline Betz Addie, Wimbledon winner and four times U. S. Women's national champion.

another. At the end of the swing your weight should be on the right foot, with the left toe still retaining contact with the ground. Straighten your elbow as you hit the ball and finish with your arm extended. Don't forget to move completely through the ball and pivot your hips and shoulders and finish with the racket pointing towards the right corner of the court.

ONE POINT AT A TIME

There are so many ingredients of a good backhand that it is impossible to think of everything and still move and hit the ball at the proper spot in relation to your body. After telling someone—change your grip, wrist firm, elbow close to body, more backswing, stay away from the ball, don't let the ball get too deep, start racket head low, keep face of racket flat, swing inside out, swing from your back, let that arm straighten out at finish, finish high—I usually hear, "let's hit forehands." The best thing to do is to concentrate on one or two points at a time so that certain motions become automatic. As you repeat the backhand swing time and again, it will become more natural to you. Honest!

Dave Shaw of Pompano Beach, Florida, has an excellent method of getting his pupils into a good hitting position. He advocates "follow the ball with your shoulder." As the ball approaches, the shoulder, also back and hips, (but not head!) should turn away which insures a good backswing. You want one motion with the racket starting past center, past the spot where the racket would point directly to back fence. I like to swing with a pupil since many times, no matter how clearly you think you are phrasing your instruction, the swing remains a jerky composite of the correct motions.

FOOTWORK

Footwork for the backhand is also just the reverse of the forehand. For both strokes you should be balanced on the balls of the feet ready to move in any direction but when you start for a backhand, step out with the left foot. For short distances, pull the right foot up to the left, starting your racket back at the same time, and turn back onto the left foot as you approach the ball. With more court to cover you'll take off like a sprinter but finish with the same pivot. I once asked a student in tennis camp, "where do you try to contact the ball"? She looked at me in utter amazement and replied, "why, where it comes, of course." As your game progresses you'll find that anticipation and footwork will let *you* determine the point of contact. There won't be so many of those extremely difficult high backhands since you will learn to get behind the bounce of the ball (it will come down, you know) and move into a waist high shot.

THE BACKHAND CHOP

You should later learn a backhand chop to handle high balls or extremely fast shots which give you no opportunity to get your racket back in position. But wait until you have a grooved flat backhand and then add the spin for convenience, variety and safety. Too many people learn a defensive chop and are unable to then change to an aggressive forcing backhand. The chop is hit with racket face open, elbow bent and leading, wrist firm and ahead of racket face.

You may despair of EVER learning a decent backhand but you will eventually feel less spastic when swinging on the left side. Slap a few hands, throw a few rackets, hit thousands and thousands of balls, practice on a backboard and you, too, may one day start running around your forehand.

Arthur Ashe stretches out to hit a backhand volley.

BACKHAND SUMMARY AND TESTS

1. MUST have eyes closed

2. Racket too small

3. Shoes too heavy

4. Takes ball too close to body

5. Racket head above wrist when hitting low balls

6. Leads with elbow

7. Faces net at start of swing

8. Wrist not firm

9. Cuts across ball

10. Too short a backswing

11. Faulty footwork

12. Hits ball too easily

13. Tries to kill every shot

14. ADDITIONAL FAULTS NO ONE ELSE HAS THOUGHT OF:

PRO'S SUGGESTIONS _____

15.

16.

17.

18.

19.

SCORES _____

Make the same five tests that you made for the forehand and see just how steady you are.

Test 1.

Test 2.

Test 3.

Test 4.

Test 5.

CHAPTER III
The Serve

Arthur Ashe hitting an American Twist serve. Notice the torn up condition of the grass court.

Most beginners find it a definite handicap to be obliged to serve every other game. We find in our tennis camp that it is very difficult for our starting groups to finish their matches since each player loses his serve with remarkable consistency. The two game margin necessary for victory is rarely achieved. Fortunately the Van Alen Tie Breaker came along and saved the day.

The serve is that overhead swing which Gonzales smashes at 125 miles per hour and young Roscoe Tanner has been clocked even faster, 130. But you'll start out at 12. The basic rule of all sports is—"Get off first." That's why the big serve is at once so desired, the most dramatic part of the whole game. To a man, a big serve is a tremendous advantage and almost a necessity, since one service break often means a lost set. The girls, in this case the weaker sex, do not usually possess such powerful serves—although there are exceptions such as Australia's Margaret Smith Court. Many have merely a pitty pat method of putting the ball in play. Boys say a girl's change of pace means slow to slower.

I was taught to serve by first throwing a ball over the net into the alternate service court. I really knew how to throw but had never realized that the throwing and serving motions were virtually identical. Of course, many girls throw "like a girl" and that is why boys find it easier and more natural to develop a hard serve.

THE GRIP

The grip should be around about as far as for the backhand but when I used to insist that every one begin with that grip, my pupils always cried "but, I can't hit it that way." And they couldn't. By all means try it and you may be one of the few who can master it right away. If not, start with the forehand grip and when you have grooved the toss and the swing, concentrate on shifting to the correct grip.

THE TOSS

The toss is another area which leads to frustration. The timing should be perfect. Place both hands together by your right side (later you'll probably start with the racket head higher) and move them directly away from each other, the left hand tossing the ball and the right hand simultaneously starting to drop the racket back by your side as if you were starting the backswing to throw the racket. By the time the ball reaches the peak of the toss, your elbow should be bent, right arm cocked ready to throw. You want to be prepared to hit the ball just as it starts down. TRY to get a consistent toss to a spot

Margaret Smith Court demonstrates American Twist Serve. She's currently making a brilliant comeback after time off to have a baby.

Clark Taylor demonstrates serve. The hands have moved apart with the left hand tossing the ball and the racket starting back.

The ball has almost reached the peak of the toss while the racket is still moving back to get into position on the shoulder.

The arm is cocked with the elbow in the same position as if the server were going to throw a baseball overhand.

43

For a flat serve, the ball is tossed slightly forward and about in line with the right shoulder.

The force of the swing should pull the right side into the court

The finish of the serve. Racket is past the left side, weight has shifted to the right foot.

slightly forward (towards the net) and as high above your head as your racket will reach when you are standing on your toes.

THE STROKE

When you feel semi-confident about the toss, try hitting the ball. Stand slightly sideways with your feet and body in the same position you would take preparing to make that overhand baseball throw. Meet the ball just below the peak of the toss with arm extended and let the racket move out towards the net before coming across the body and down past your left side. Your weight should be shifting forward as you bring your racket through, and at the moment of impact the racket face should be flat against the ball. If you're now using the backhand grip you'll have to make a wrist turn or you'll slice the ball to the left. The wrist snap to hit the ball is the same as when releasing a baseball.

PRACTICE

Sound complicated? It's even worse when you're out on the court. At least, the service is easy to practice since you don't have to scour the neighborhood for an opponent. Try to round up those 25 balls you used for the forehand and backhand tests. (Fewer are required if you can locate a small boy, or cooperative small dog, to act as a retriever.) Ultimately, you'll have to aim. If you've wondered about those squares in the forecourt on the opposite side of the net, those are the service courts. Stand just to the right of center behind the baseline and hit the ball diagonally over the net into the deuce court. Next, move to the left of center and practice into what you'll later learn is called the ad or advantage court. If you find every serve hitting the net, move your toss back a little. If they're all going deep, or between the service line and the baseline, you probably should move the ball forward or, possibly, you're meeting the ball when it is too low and your serve takes off like a line drive. The depth of the serve depends upon the angle of the racket face on contact.

If you do everything right, with the proper timing, (most un-likely!) serving should pull your right foot into the court at the END of the swing. Don't just step in arbitrarily because everybody else is doing it. Wait until you feel that pull on your right side and then let the foot swing over the line.

VARIATIONS

Some professionals teach a slice serve before the more powerful flat service. The toss is lower and to the right and the hit is across and around the outside of the ball. The slice is easier to control (once you learn it) and makes a good, safe second serve. Yes, you get two chances on the serve.

The serve that you see on television, used by the pros and ranking amateurs, is called the American Twist. They look as if they're about to fall backwards on their heads or possibly break their backs. Don't try it until you feel fairly secure with the flat serve since the ball must be thrown behind your head and you've undoubtedly knocked yourself out learning to toss it in front of you. Hit hard across the ball from left to right and swing up and over the ball. Pros differ in their advice as to the finish but I prefer the finish on the right side. It won't seem difficult—merely impossible. And don't give up just because you hit the ball on the edge of the racket and kite it over the fence at a direct right angle. You're on the right track.

STRATEGY

The server may be likened to a baseball pitcher who studies each batter to decide which pitch will be least expected and most disliked. It is not always good judgment to direct the ball to an inferior backhand as the receiver will be waiting there and covering only half the court. An occasional flat serve to the forehand will keep him in the center of the service court so that he will have to reach for a wide backhand instead of already being in the perfect position. A tall player many times has difficulty with a serve bouncing into his body, while it is relatively easy for him to reach for the wide shots.

Many beginners, especially you big strong ones, immediately try to serve the ball as hard as possible. You're like some men golfers who are sublimely happy to knock an occasional drive out past everyone else despite the fact that the majority of their drives come to rest two fairways away. Learn a rhythmic, sound swing first and the power will come, along with the necessary control. I remember when I was playing a practice match at a resort and a non-tennis-playing guest wanted me to explain why I always hit one ball into the net before starting to serve. I belatedly realized that having perfected a safe second serve, I tried to hit such a hard, flat service that I never got it over the net. So, if you're emulating my "once into the net before serving," better ease up or give yourself a greater margin of safety.

There are advantages, other than speed, in hitting your first serve in the court. Your opponent is never quite so set and ready for play and, expecting a hard, deep ball, will not be playing close enough to make an aggressive return of what would normally be your slower second delivery. Even when someone is hitting identical first and second services to me I always have much more confidence returning the second ball. Always hesitate between the first and second services and try to analyze why the first serve missed. Try a different toss, a different stance or a more deliberate, safer swing. Don't go through exactly the same motions and wonder why you serve so many double faults.

Any server who is able to hit a fairly hard, well-placed ball possesses a great advantage, irrespective of the number of aces he may serve. First, he puts the ball in play from the center of his own court, while the receiver is already far to the left or right and will probably be drawn even farther out of position. He is initially able to place the ball to his opponent's weak side, and he is allowed the margin of serving two balls while the receiver is entitled to only one error. Hardly seems fair! Since the service is the first ball hit, it will be the first offensive stroke, and the return in most cases will be a defensive shot. When you learn to dash to the net and volley off a weak return for an outright winner, you have a definite asset in a big serve. Rushing the net behind the serve is exciting but it's not such a thrill to see the ball whizzing by on either side of you. Don't attempt that mad dash until you've had a few volleying lessons.

When Maurice McLoughlin, the famed California Comet, came out of the west with his flaming hair and cheerful grin, he captured the tennis world with his mighty service, and his lusty wallops brought about a new era in tennis. There were many who marvelled and said that his like would not pass their way again. His serve sizzled like—had the term been proper in those days—a jet plane. Halley's Comet was better known then, and a "comet" the Californian became.

Of course his serve was mighty and the gallery loved it—as crowds love the display of power and punch in any sport. But many another tremendous server came along to smack the ball with such abandon that it looked like a mothball zooming over the net. There were the great hitters like Tilden and Budge and Vines and Kramer and Gonzales and Laver and Ashe and now, Roscoe Tanner. Perhaps in the men's division there will come along a superman who will win by all aces.

SERVICE SUMMARY AND TESTS

1. It doesn't go in the court
2. Toss too low
3. Net too darn high
4. Toss and racket motion not synchronized
5. No elbow bend
6. No wrist snap
7. Racket finishes on right side
8. Racket finishes on left side but too far out from body
9. Hits down on ball
10. Obviously never played baseball

PRO'S SUGGESTIONS

11.

12.

13.

14.

15.

SCORES

Test 1. Try hitting 10 serves into the left hand court and 10 into the right. Check your progress weekly. As you get stronger and more proficient you can make the tests with more and more balls.

Test 2. Practice your serves as first and second serves to see how many double faults you would serve.

John Newcombe starting into net behind his serve.

CHAPTER IV
Volley, Overhead Smash, Lob and Drop Shot

Susie Glutz herself.

When Sarah Palfrey Danzig and I went on a nation-wide professional tour we played at numerous schools and colleges. We wanted to give some instruction without putting the audiences to sleep. Out of our dilemma came the idea of Susie Glutz—me—and straight woman and teacher—Sarah. I stumbled onto the court clad in drooping size forty men's shorts, a sloppy sweat shirt dyed a nauseating orange, large black basketball shoes, no socks, a rain hat and carrying a broken racket warped to the shape of a spoon. I managed to disregard Milton Berle's advice when he caught our act at Grossinger's and advised me to black out my front teeth. Susie Glutz even made TV, although one of the cameramen wanted to know if I intended to play or plough.

THE VOLLEY

When Sarah straightened me out on my groundstrokes and reached the point of teaching me to volley, Susie's indignant reply was "That's the way I was playing before you made me stop pushing the ball and changed my game all around." In other words, when you start to volley, hitting the ball in the air before it bounces, you should forget about your newly acquired classic backswing and follow through and simply control the ball with a short punch and a locked wrist. You'll be near the net hitting the ball and you don't need lengthy strokes. Stand at least a yard from the net when you practice volleying.

The backhand and forehand volleys should be hit with the same grips as your respective ground strokes, although there are many fine players who volley with the same grip both forehand and backhand. If you wait in the ready position, throat (of racket) resting in the left hand, practice will enable you to get the racket back and change to the correct grip automatically and in a fraction of a second.

Turn to the side to volley, although many times you will not have time to move the left foot forward for a forehand or the right for a backhand. At least, pivot your hips and shoulders around so that there is some semblance of being sideways.

In doubles, particularly, volleying is almost entirely racket work since the exchanges are at too close quarters to allow for much foot or body action. When the ball is hit directly at you, don't panic and dive for the ground, or freeze and get hit in the eye. Many a placement has been inadvertently made by the player who gets that racket up fast to protect himself.

Rusty Addie demonstrates forehand volley. The left foot has crossed over, racket head is high and slightly open and wrist is ahead.

Backhand volley. Now the right foot has crossed over and shoulders have turned.

A low forehand volley. Notice that the knees are bent, racket face very open with the head of the racket touching the ground.

It's not great form, but Ken Rosewall rarely misses an overhead.

Keep your racket level with the flight of the ball, head of racket slightly above the wrist, and LEARN to volley with the face slightly open so that you chop the ball. When the ball is higher than the net it is possible and not too difficult to hit down on the ball with the racket face flat. But wait until you have mastered the chop volley before blasting away. For both forehand and backhand, try to meet the ball in front of the body.

THE DROP VOLLEY

The drop volley is a delicate touch shot which is generally in use only among advanced players. Althea Gibson made good use of this volley, which drops barely over the net and makes your opponent almost fall on his face trying to reach it. I like beginners to concentrate on it since it forces them to volley easily, almost with a blocking motion, and keeps the wrist firm and ahead.

The first woman in America to use the volley effectively was Hazel Hotchkiss Wightman, donor of the famous cup for international women's competition which bears her name. Mrs. Wightman had the advantage of several tennis playing brothers and she developed their aggressive type of volleying, which was considered too un-genteel for the women of her day. After her came many other great women volleyers such as Alice Marble, Sarah Palfrey, Margaret Osborne duPont, Louise Brough Clapp, Darlene Hard, Maria Bueno, Doris Hart and Billie Jean King. It became standard operating procedure to include the volley in your tennis equipment if you hoped to become a champion.

I always felt that I had a good volley but I couldn't prove it since whenever I rushed the net the ball went past instead of to me. Therefore, I felt more at home on the baseline where I was the one executing the passing shots. And certainly I had good company in preferring to be a backcourt player: the great Helen Wills Moody, the late "Little Mo" Connolly who became our National Champion at the age of 16, Nancy Richey Gunter and Chris Evert are all far better behind the baseline than at the net.

I have often wondered just what is the secret of being an outstanding volleyer—fast reflexes, a quick eye, a strong wrist, good anticipation? Yes, but any top player has these attributes, and yet many steady back-court stars never excel at the net. Perhaps there are other things—a touch of impatience, so that the player is not content to rally but wants to get to the net where the point is either won or lost

"Little Mo" Connolly approaches the net.

more quickly; an aggressive court spirit, with the competitor wanting to control and dominate the play; a desire to be sensational, as no one denies that the ground stroking perfectionist appears dull indeed compared to the dashing volleyer. At any rate, to volley well you must prefer the net position to any other, and once there, have a feeling of security and confidence.

The volleyer in men's tennis was unknown when the game began to spread in the 1880's. A stiff-collared young man named Oliver S. Campbell went to Newport, R.I., for the American championship, and was eliminated by Henry W. Slocum who roughly corresponded to the title holder—although in those days competitive tennis was more of a clique affair and didn't draw players from all parts of the country.

Mr. Campbell was defeated by Mr. Slocum and promptly decided that he must do more volleying and less playing from the backcourt. So Mr. Campbell hit upon the brilliant theory of running in on his service and continually staying at the net. This was considered a radical departure from accepted play, but Campbell so proved his theory that by the turn of the century, every leading player had adopted the volley, and it was conceded that only a fairly good volleyer could ever hope to win championship honors.

In top flight men's tennis, except possibly on very slow clay courts, a good volley is an absolute necessity. In women's tennis, I'm not convinced. But then, I was a guard in basketball, center half or goalie in hockey (the last line of defense), and I could never stand the thought that once that tennis ball went past me, the point was irrevocably lost. In the backcourt I've always felt that no matter where the ball was placed, somehow I'd get there and make the return. This idea found me stretched out on the ground numerous times but I certainly made more than my share of "impossible gets," and I still love to run just for the sheer joy of running.

THE LOB

Not only can the ball be hit past you when you're at the net, but there's also a fiendish shot called a "lob" when your opponent, especially when you're looking right into the sun, hits the ball high over your head. You were probably lobbing the ball back and forth before you started lessons as this is the way most youngsters begin. Prepare for the lob almost as though you were going to hit a ground stroke, but open the face of the racket in order to change the trajectory of the ball. Start the racket head low and finish high. You'll have to practice in order to determine how hard you can hit and still keep the ball in the court. A lob is useful when you are far out of court and need a shot which will allow you time to get back into position.

THE OVERHEAD SMASH

As the other fellow is also learning to lob, you'll have to counteract it by learning the overhead smash, also known, in moments of stress, by other names.

Theoretically, anyone who is able to serve well automatically possesses a good overhead, since the swings are virtually the same. Most of the problems of the overhead come not from the swing but from the attempt to anticipate and judge the position of the ball. Beginners tend to let the ball drop too low and by the time they swing, the ball is hitting them on the head.

FOOTWORK

Usually, you'll have to move backwards to reach the lob. Start with the right foot but turn sideways as you skip backwards so that your left side will be to the net as you smash. Get your racket back quickly, cock your arm and bend your elbow as you do for the serve and try to contact the ball when it's about a foot in front of your head in line with the right eye. You want to meet it high enough so that your arm can stretch out, just as in a serve. Hit down and over the top of the ball with plenty of wrist snap. Let the racket follow through past your left side. Many times you'll have to jump off the ground as you smash.

If the ball seems to be coming directly down on you from a vast height, the best method of handling it is to let it bounce and then attempt to smash it away. It's no more cowardly than signaling for a fair catch in football when seven or eight Washington Redskins are looking down your throat. There's a definite safety factor involved in both cases.

STRATEGY

When you find a boy or girl who is steady as a rock in the backcourt but who has an inadequate volley or overhead, your objective should be to draw him to the net. This can be accomplished by hitting

When hitting a lob, note the same footwork as used in normal forehand except that the face of the racket is much more open.

the ball short. If the ball sits up too high, however, he can probably run up and put it away without finding it necessary to use his weak volley. The drop shot is the best method for breaking up the rhythm of a sound baseline game.

THE DROP SHOT

A good drop shot, just clearing the net, is a winner. A bad one is suicidal. I lost so many points learning the drop shot that I finally decided the only time to use one was when my opponent was deep behind the baseline with one foot caught under the fence. At least, you want to be in the forecourt with your opponent behind the baseline so that the ball will have the short distance to cover and your opponent the longer. It is not enough to merely hit the ball more easily in order to make it barely clear the net. A drop shot is a definite and distinct stroke which should be learned and practiced. Some players complain that they have no "touch" but, like card sense, it can be acquired. Neither a drop shot nor a dummy reversal is automatic.

While a ground stroke should normally be hit with the racket face flat, a drop shot is actually a chop with almost no follow through.

The drop shot is hit very much like the drop volley (except that the ball has bounced) with the face of the racket open to impart under spin and help the ball "die." Try letting the ball get fairly deep on both drop volleys and drop shots. All chop strokes are hit with the ball coming into you more than your flat shots. Don't follow through or you'll keep that ball moving towards your opponent, which is hardly your objective. Bend your elbow, keep your wrist firm and ahead of the racket face, and be selective as to who is on the other side of the net when you employ the drop shot. Girls and anyone over 50 (except Bobby Riggs) are naturals.

I once tried to teach a drop shot to Mrs. Eunice Kennedy Shriver. She is quite a good player with sound ground strokes and I explained how she could add some variety to her game. She was rather astounded at the drop shot and said, "No wonder you were the champion." I'm not at all sure that she thought its use would be completely ethical in her circles.

Volley, overhead, lob, or drop shot—these are not intricate shots merely for the champions. You'll develop a better game once you get some expert help on their execution from a qualified professional.

64

SUMMARY AND TESTS

Volley

1. Racket head follows through too far
2. Faces Net
3. Lets Ball Get Too Deep
4. Wrist Collapses
5. And what else?

Overhead

6. Lets Ball Drop Too Low
7. Doesn't Stand Sideways
8. Too Fancy and Long a Windup
9. No Follow Through

PRO'S SUGGESTIONS

10.
11.
12.
13.
14.

Have Someone Hit You 25 Forehand Volleys
SCORES

Test 1. Number hit in net————
Test 2. Number hit over baseline————
Test 3. Number hit in court————
Test 4. Number of times ball glanced off wood and hit you in the mouth ————
Test 5. Now repeat with the backhand volley and put scores next to those for the forehand volley.

CHAPTER V
Clothing and Equipment

Jimmy Connors makes the shot with his metal racket. He has a two-handed back-hand even for his volley!

You remember the famous remark about the late writer, Heywood Broun: "He looked like an unmade bed." That's the way some people can look—even with the most expensive clothes.

This is by no means a fashion critique. But it is almost impossible to look other than athletic, trim, and glamorous in tennis clothes—assuming you have been blessed with the normal allotment of a couple of legs, two arms and a body which performs reasonably gracefully. You don't even have to play well to gain the respect of the onlookers. Put on your beautiful cable stitch English imported sweater and drop a few casual remarks such as "cross court forehand", "center court" or "as I was saying to Arthur Ashe the other day" and everyone will assume that you're a circuit player.

CHANGES IN SPORTS FASHIONS

Fashions change in all sports. In the early days of football, a head full of hair, such as the Beatles affect, was the best shock absorber for a blow. (You see, things have a way of coming full cycle because the styles of the 1880's in football now are popular again, this time for guitar players.)

Baseball players once wore high button collars and some of the early dandies even wore ties to go along with their sideburns and mustaches. The 1972 World Champion Oakland Athletics proved that the old mod style is no deterrent to a championship club.

Golfers used to wear something called "knickers" or "plus-fours". Look at some of the old pictures of the great golfers. They wore short pants, shirts, ties and jackets. Colorful comfort is the rule now on the links.

The same unsubtle transformation has taken place in tennis. The dolls and guys of the 1890's looked like astronauts stuffed in space suits. The girls wore those long dresses which must have been designed by an expert on cow catchers. I suppose the courts never needed sweeping after these gals were through playing a match.

But time marches on and long dresses gave way to shorts and skirts and now to very short dresses. The men's heavy long flannels have been replaced by cooler and more comfortable shorts. Tennis is a game associated with girls and boys, men and women, dressed immaculately in white, although Head and several other companies are making some beautiful pastel dresses. Many clubs will still not allow other than white clothing although it is customary to view Arthur Ashe in blue or yellow, Newcombe in red, and Graebner in pink. It seems that the pros are trying their best to abolish the traditionally white tennis requirement.

The only time I've deviated from all white was when I made a professional tour with "Gorgeous Gussy" Moran. Gussy had been a sensation at Wimbledon with her "lace panties" and before we opened at Madison Square Garden in New York the newspapers were full of speculation as to what Gussy would wear. There was little space left to mention that Jack Kramer, Pancho Segura and I would also be playing. Determined not to be totally eclipsed, I had my own wardrobe made up and when the big night arrived, I appeared in silver lame shorts, a shocking pink sweater and large hair ribbon to match. Gussy, surprisingly, appeared in white and *Time* Magazine headlined "the Big Switch." I also had leopard and zebra skin shorts, plus purple, orange and the gold lame popularized by Miami's beautiful Karol Fageros, and it's too bad I was ahead of color TV. Gussy had been ranked fourth in the country but her strokes were overshadowed by her glamour girl publicity and I don't feel that she was ever given enough credit as an excellent tennis player.

COST OF TENNIS CLOTHES

You ladies can and do spend a fortune on tennis dresses, ranging from $15 to $50 from such dress makers as Agile, Allie Mae, American Golfer, Mondessa, Loom Togs, Match Point, Timandra, Spairistike and Head. For the men, double knit shorts are popular, and Perry (Wimbledon Wreath emblem—$12 from Carl Fix) and LaCoste (Alligator emblem—$14 from Izod) are among the best selling shirts. The Spalding Gonzales is a good cheaper shirt at $6 and terrylene shorts at $20 by Simpson, Perry or LaCoste are worn by many of the touring pros.

Both men and women have become enamoured of the warm-up suit. Once seen only on the early morning jogger, now the indoor and outdoor tennis player has his nylon or cotton warm-up suits in white (with a blue stripe), blue (with a white stripe), navy, orange, or red. They're made by White Stag, Add-In, Adidas, SAI and Court Casual and cost from $20 to $45.

TENNIS SHOES

Shoes should be white and low cut, either the oxford type or laced to the toe (no basketball shoes). Tretorn also has beige and blue which seem to be gaining in popularity. You have a wide selection of shoes from which to choose; Ours, Adidas, Head, Puma and Tretorn (distributed by Bancroft)—all have canvas or leather top tennis shoes. Converse, distributed by Wilson, has a good arch and the retail cost should be from $12 to $13 for the canvas shoes. The Tretorn canvas

Silver lame, shocking pink, and victory against Gussie Moran at Madison Square Garden.

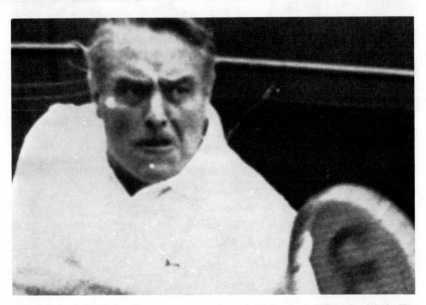

The form here doesn't do justice to R. Sargent Shriver's excellent forehand. His wife, Eunice Kennedy Shriver, and sister-in-law, Ethel Kennedy, are also very good players.

70

They used to play tennis dressed like this!

More up-to-date tennis fashions . . .

is very comfortable and costs $15—its leather is about $25. Adidas, Puma and Head all have a good quality leather shoe costing from $18 to $20.

Socks should be fairly thick, either cotton, wool, nylon or some combination. Stretch socks are made in most materials though I once tried to sell a man on the advantage of having "socks for the entire family" and he replied: "That's an advantage?" Cost—$1 to $3.50. The ladies seem to prefer the peds (half-sox) for $1.60 which prevents that line around the ankle.

BUYING A RACKET

How do I pick out the right racket? Probably the right answer to that often asked question is that realistically there is no one "right" racket for you. A professional can help you select the proper weight and handle size but can only make suggestions as to the make of racket. You'll have to decide that on the basis of price, appearance and feel. You can pay somewhere from $6 or $7 for a pre-strung Pakistanian or Japanese import or around $58 for the frame of a Head aluminum Competition.

METAL VS. WOOD

The metal frame has its advantages and disadvantages. First—the bad news! Steel and aluminum, whether Wilson, Spalding, Slazenger, Revere, Chemhold, Head or Seamless—all tend to make it harder to control the ball than do the wood frames. The Wilson T-2000 has rather a sling shot effect although the newer T-3000 with an insert across the throat does add to its stability. The beginner or the steady player is undoubtedly better off with wood. You can also endanger life, limb, and teeth if you hit yourself with a metal racket.

And now—the good news! The metal frames are relatively lighter, easier to handle, make for harder serves, more power and put more punch (frequently over the baseline) into your volleys. Shots which you barely reach can be more easily flicked by metal than by wood. Theoretically the racket is longer lasting but actually each company continues to have problems while constantly trying to improve its metal frames. The grommets break or come out so that the racket has to be patched or stringing replaced much more often than with wood. (That's back to the bad news.) The metal racket makers claim their product is good for preventing tennis elbow but I acquired that dreaded and much discussed ailment while playing with aluminum and got rid of it with a combination of cortisone and wood.

The Classic I and Classic II, $40, made by Davis for Victor Sports, Inc., combine the springiness of metal with the steady qualities of wood. The resiliency of the Classic frames comes from Classidon, a substance discovered in the space program. Bancroft has a racket called the F R S ($35) which contains fiber glass and is also a fine playing frame.

The various companies present a complete line of rackets, ranging from $8 to $10 for a pre-strung racket to $22 or $35 or $40 for frame only. You might think you have a great buy when you say you found a Wilson Kramer for $10 but he has his name on both low end and top "Autograph" rackets in the line. You'll get about what you pay for so don't buy the name. It doesn't necessarily mean that by using a Gonzales autograph your serve will increase in velocity or that the Budge autograph comes with a built-in backhand.

You'll pay less if you buy a factory strung racket but make sure that it has been strung fairly well. Test the tightness of the stringing by hitting (gently) another racket against it. If it doesn't have a high pitch—forget it. You'll need all the help you can get. Start out with as good a racket as you can afford—at least to the level of a nylon strung Davis Hi-Point, around $22. DON'T dig out one from the closet and announce cheerfully that it hasn't even been used for 20 years. Spalding has come up with a well-made new wood and fiberglass frame which retails for $49.50.

The majority of the good players use a frame which costs around $22 to $25. Wilson has its autograph frames, Budge, Kramer, Smith and Richey; Spalding the Gonzales plus Doris Hart for the ladies; Dunlop has its made in England Maxply; the up-and-coming Seamless Co. has its Rosewall; Bancroft, Slazenger, Pennsylvania, Garcia—all have excellent top frames. Davis has its beautiful (seven layers of enamel make their frames appear to be inlaid wood) Imperials and Tads. Of course, you're not through once you buy the frame. Something must go in the middle unless you expect to be hitting the majority of shots on the wood.

NYLON VS. GUT

Nylon is a synthetic which plays substantially the same as gut. It will not "hold" the ball quite so well but is quite adequate for all except top flight players. It will cost from $8 to $10, including the stringing charge, for monofilament to vantage.

Gut is beef or lamb so forget all the gags about the little kitten watching the tennis match and crying because his mommy was in the racket. Make that a little lamb! Victor Imperial is the top name in the gut field and will cost you about $20 including stringing charge. Victor has less expensive gut and almost every big company either makes or distributes gut. It will generally out last nylon and if you have or are expecting "tennis elbow," by all means invest in gut as it will be easier on your arm. If you use a lot of "touch shots" you'll certainly have more success with the extra feel of the gut strung racket.

Some gut is coated and moisture proof and with all nylon you may play in the rain. Now what could be more fun than tennis in the rain? (Especially if you wear glasses.)

If you hit the ball flat and not too hard, chances are that a string job will last you one season or more. Top spinning or cutting the ball and using an American Twist Serve are all very abrasive and you may have to restring your racket quite frequently. A cheap racket should not be restrung but the better frames can be restrung two or three times—usually. Let the pro check the frame for cracks or weakness in the head. If one or two strings have broken, these may be replaced at about 75 cents per string but again, follow the advice of the professional. Patching generally causes the entire string job to loosen and, if other strings are fraying, you would probably have to have a complete restringing job soon.

A pre-strung racket probably won't require a press but any tightly strung racket should be kept in a press (about $2) to avoid warping. A cover is useful when you want to protect gut and ornamental when your racket is strung with nylon.

WHAT TO DO IF YOUR RACKET SLIPS

If you have trouble holding the racket because of perspiration you can buy sweatlets for your wrist—90 cents to $1 for 2. S. A. I. makes them in all colors, as well as headbands (80 cents). S. A. I. also makes gloves, full fingered or half, about $4.50. As well as preventing slipping, the tennis glove will help avoid blisters.

Some players reverse the handle on the racket. The good frames have leather grips and the pro can turn it for you so that the rough side is out. You can buy a new leather grip when the old one seems too slippery ($3 to $4 including installation). There are handles of toweling material and most pro shops sell small rosin bags.

TENNIS BALLS

They don't come in quite all sizes and shapes (most are round) but they now come in many colors and makes. You can buy balls in white, fuscia and fluorescent yellow—the yellow being especially popular for indoor visibility. There are several major tennis ball manufacturers. General Tire Co. which makes the Pennsylvania, Wilson and Bancroft balls; Dunlop Rubber Co. which has added an Australian made ball to its line due to the tremendous demand for tennis balls this past two years; Spalding which makes the Spalding and Wright-Ditson; Slazenger (made in England) which makes the Slazenger and Seamless. The Pennsylvania Sporting Goods Co. distributes the Maxima and Phillips balls which are made in England. Sweden produced the Tretorn (distributed by Bancroft) which is non-pressurized and long lasting.

Tennis balls are sold in threes and come in a vacuum sealed can which will screw open, pop open, snap open or NOT open, the latter when you are far from civilization and things such as screw drivers or can openers. They are made to slightly different specifications but all the top balls conform to the United States Lawn Tennis Association standards. A can sells for $2.50 to $3 and going up. Some of the companies put out a cheaper ball which may sell for under $2 but starts out slightly dead.

Tennis balls should retain their life and be good for three sets—your kids can use them another three—and the dog, indefinitely.

John Newcombe, three-time Wimbledon champion, holds aloft his 1971 Wimbledon trophy.

Betz-Taylor tennis camp at Sidwell Friends School, Washington, D.C.

Television star Dan Rowan and wife play mixed doubles with professionals Pauline Betz Addie and Clark Taylor.

Lefty Rod Laver leaps off the ground to hit an overhead smash.

CHAPTER VI
Strategy for Singles and Doubles

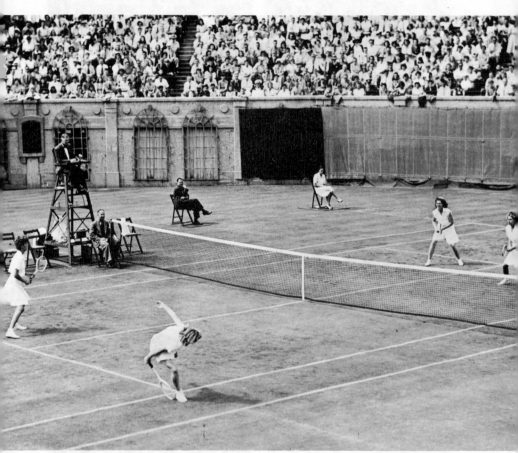

Pauline in action at the Forest Hills Stadium with Doris Hart against Louise Brough Clapp and Margaret Osborne duPont.

Now that you have a forehand, backhand, service, volley, over-head lob and drop shot, who can possibly beat you? Practically every-body! That is, until you know how to use your strokes.

Sometimes you can watch two players in a match and not know which one is winning (although usually it's the one who's smiling). One player is hitting beautiful shots and the other scrambling around just getting the ball back. You conclude that the one with the picture swings must be the better player, but find out that he's getting clob-bered. You should work hard to get the correct strokes since this is the way to gain consistency, but don't go all out for form and go down swinging.

There are two ways for you to win a point—by a placement on your part or by a welcome error from your opponent. The most aggravating type of opponent is the one who gets everything back and I feel that the starting player should adopt this aggravating style of game. Play well within your capabilities. It is enough to play steady tennis and keep the ball fairly deep. Don't be sensitive when your defeated embittered opponent derisively calls you a "pusher." The big hitters of today were the pushers of yesterday and you won't be con-demning yourself to a tennis lifetime of merely keeping the ball in play.

DON'T BEAT YOURSELF

Once you have learned ball control, you can get on with the place-ment method of winning points. Don't try to make a winner of every shot. You want to build up to a placement by hitting deep shots to your opponent, or perhaps wide angles, until he hits an easy return which you will be able to put away with some degree of safety. Far too many matches are lost by players beating themselves—that is, with the majority of points lost by unforced errors.

Experience will teach you which shot is a good risk and which will succeed only once in ten attempts. The odds are definitely against your making an ace from far behind the base line, and in favor of your putting away a set-up in the forecourt. Don't aim for the lines or try to skim the ball a half inch over the net. Give yourself a reason-able margin of safety.

Consider both your own and your opponent's game. If someone is outsteadying you from the backcourt, obviously a change is indicated. It is relatively easy to run from side to side, so try to break up your opponent's game by an occasional midcourt shot or try to draw him to the net by drop-shotting. A short crosscourt followed by a deep shot to the opposite corner usually proves effective. Playing your own game is a good idea only when it is a winning one. Don't go down to defeat and console yourself with the thought that "he couldn't make me change my game." However, analyze why you are losing before making too drastic a change.

If you are a player noted for steadiness, don't immediately resign yourself to the fact that you can't win from the backcourt and think that you have nothing to lose by going to the net every point and trying for winners. If your ground strokes are going out, try steadying them down by adding a little top spin and then go back to hitting flat shots as you gain more control.

On the other hand, if you are ordinarily a good volleyer but in this particular match the passing shots are whizzing by with monotonous regularity, try hitting harder and deeper approach shots before deciding that this is the time to stay back and work on an erratic forehand.

COPY THE CHAMPS

It is natural that the rising young players should attempt to imitate the current champions. The girls, watching the great Billie Jean King, Rosie Casals and Evonne Goolagong tend to concentrate on volleying, to the detriment of their ground strokes. A reliable forehand and backhand should remain the most important part of a women's stroking equipment so that she can rally until a short ball is hit and there is a good opportunity to go to the net. Margaret Smith Court, is a fine volleyer but she also has sound ground strokes. I once watched her play a match in Florida against her fellow Australian, Leslie Turner, and was amazed by the power, the depth and the consistency of the forehands and backhands of both girls.

So the answer is to be proficient both at the net and in the backcourt. It is foolish to go to the net when the odds are against you and equally foolish to remain in the backcourt when you could make a forcing shot off a short ball and have every chance of making a successful volley.

Don't follow your serve to the net unless you have a fine serve, an excellent volley, or possibly an easily intimidated opponent who makes a weak return every time you charge the barrier. Somehow the net man acts as a magnet when he first appears and it takes quite a while to get the idea that you're to hit past and not to him.

Our big stars such as Ken Rosewall, Stan Smith, Arthur Ashe, John Newcombe, Rod Laver and Bob Lutz, can make the ball break so far with their American Twist serves that their opponents often find themselves completely off the court when making their return, giving every advantage to the man coming in. Also, the high bounce to the right means that the receiver is many times returning serve with a high backhand, which is, for most players, the game's most difficult shot. One answer to a good American Twist service is to move in and hit it before it has a chance to kick high or to the side. However, only a very good player is able to do this consistently.

If you practice enough against a hard flat serve, you'll develop a blocking method of returning the ball. You will find it impossible to stroke any ball hit extremely hard right into you and will instead be forced to block or chop the ball to consistently keep it in play.

The good men volleyers chip the ball when they go into net. If you watch the great Australians, Rod Laver, Roy Emerson or the other top pros and amateurs you'll notice that they rarely hit cross court on an approach shot but usually go in behind a down-the-line or straight shot.

Actually, I feel that by the time you have played the game of tennis for a few years, your strategy is almost automatic. Many times when I was commended for clever thinking and strategy I had no remembrance of consciously changing my game. Eventually, strategy becomes more instinct than thought.

DOUBLES

There are many differences in both style and strategy between singles and doubles play. The big advantage of playing doubles is that after losing a match you no longer have to blame your defeat upon adverse weather conditions, a late night, bad ice, slippery court, or unfair decisions. You simply explain that your partner was a little off his game. And you need suffer no pangs of conscience, since you can be assured that your partner is making the reverse explanation to his circle of friends.

Women's doubles used to be the signal for the audience to rise en masse and go out to tea. When the volley came into more constant use, even the girls began to play a more interesting game of doubles as they progressed from a baseline battle to an occasional rally at the

"I'll take it, Pancho!" Pauline and Gonzales are playing an exhibition against two men.

net. For years, the usual formation was the dangerous one up and one back—the server rarely following in to the net. Unless the partners remain parallel, they are almost defenseless against a diagonal shot between them.

The old method undoubtedly was a bore to watch and the player at net was no more than a spectator while a base line duel went on between the opponents in the backcourt. Now, however, it is the accepted strategy for both players to rush the net at every opportunity, since most of the points are won at the net and the aggressive team is the winning combination. Steady ground strokes, speed of foot and defensive ability (That's me!) are of much less value in doubles than a sound volley and overhead (Oh!). The ability to keep the ball low and at your opponents' feet so that they will be forced to hit up to you; to follow a serve into the net behind a high bouncing twist; to keep the return of service away from the net man and in a difficult volleying position for the server—all these make the good doubles player.

When your partner is serving and you are at the net, you should cover the alley and short lobs over your head. Additionally, you should try to cover any service returns not more than two steps away. Occasionally, if you have a decent volley and an understanding partner, you should take a calculated risk and leave the alley open to dart across the net and knock off the return. This puts additional pressure on the receiver. If he seems to be consistently "out-guessing" you, the chances are that you're leaving too soon.

TEMPTATIONS OF TEAMWORK

Good teamwork is an essential. Louise Brough Clapp and Margaret Osborne duPont, with almost countless National Doubles Championships to their credit, were almost unbeatable. Both held their American Twist serves with consummate ease and they were constantly at the net presenting a solid, formidable front. You couldn't hit over them or through them. Having played together over a long period of time, they worked in perfect accord. You never saw both politely step aside yelling "yours, partner!" as the ball escaped down the middle.

Some of our great men's doubles teams have been Tilden-Richards (Richards being only 15 years old when he first played Davis-Cup Doubles with Big Bill Tilden), Lott-Stoefen, Allison-Van Ryn, Budge-Mako, Talbert-Mulloy (both still going strong), Kramer-Schroeder, Ralston-McKinley, and now Smith-Van Dillon and Okker-Riessen.

Professional Allie Ritzenberg is backed up by Gardner Mulloy

Carole (Mrs. Clark) Graebner is also an excellent doubles player and partnered Nancy Richey to the United States and Australian National Championships.

If your partner misses two set-ups in a row, don't scream out "how can I play against three opponents?" Chances are that if you do, he'll blow the next one too. Be the calm steadying influence and encourage him into better tennis. If he persists in missing set-ups, find a new partner.

Mixed doubles, or boy-girl type tennis, is great fun (at least, for the girls). I fear that some men have the same fond regard for mixed doubles as the men golfers who say that they practice for a mixed two-ball tournament by hitting one ball and kicking the next. In my day (yes, we had automobiles, radios, beginning television, talking pictures and even Cary Grant) there was a mad scramble for good mixed partners at the tournaments since you were frequently given free room and board only so long as you remained in some event.

The only place I can ever remember being much in demand as a doubles partner was at Charlie Farrell's Racquet Club in Palm Springs, California. My mixed games there were far different from a tournament mixed match where the opposing players do their best to keep the ball away from the man. I played with director Mervyn LeRoy as a partner and could never get into the action, despite my continual admonition to the opposition to "play the girl." Only Spencer Tracy, upon whom I bestowed my weak overhead, told me that I was about to become the first champion to be dropped while still champion.

Whether you're playing singles or doubles, thinking a good game of tennis won't make you a champion. In order to execute a plan, you must have the equipment, in this case the basic stroking ability, to carry through successfully. Work hard to control your strokes before deciding to be the master tactician.

COURTSMANSHIP

No discussion of tennis strategy would be complete without mentioning another aspect of the game, especially for the girls. I don't know whether Napoleon said it or not, but strategy on and off the court is knowing what to do and when. If HE finally asks you to play tennis with him, somehow you must manage to lose. I state this from experience. My reaction to masculine superiority, now termed male chauvinism, which says "No girl can beat me!" had me winning matches and losing boy friends for years until I finally captured a non-tennis player. The male ego is such that he is not about to admire you for your great backhand. He seems to like a girl who is well coordinated enough to give him some practice, but who listens respectfully as he explains how she can improve her overhead. If he's so bad that despite purposefully throwing points you find yourself at match point, sprain your ankle and let him masterfully carry you off the court.

When you're playing mixed doubles and he asks you which side you prefer, don't tell him that your backhand is better than his and that you want the advantage court. Next week (and maybe the next dance) his partner will be the girl who can't play a lick but who looks admiringly at him and sighs, "Gee, how can you hit the ball so hard?" For those further along in life and perhaps angling for a second wife or husband, I don't feel such strategy is necessarily right. He may have had it with admiring helplessness and be on the lookout for someone who can help him win the club mixed doubles.

And boys . . . don't despair if you didn't make the Little League team and you're too small for football. Either learn to kick soccer style like the football place kicking Gogolaks, or take up tennis. You will get ahead of the star athletes in the longer run if you concentrate on tennis while they're hitting baseballs or knocking each other down on the football field.

While it is undoubtedly true that tennis requires as much or more coordination and athletic ability than any other sport, it is equally true that the best and only way to become a good tennis player is by playing many years of tennis. After lessons and practice, you can make the high school quarterback look silly when you entice him to the opposite side of the net. And you can play tennis with all of the pretty girls while who, besides the Kennedy wives, can join you at football?

John Newcombe in action.

CHAPTER VII

Tournament Play

Pauline and the late Maureen Connolly get together for some 1966 exhibition matches.

The crowd is hushed now. You're on the center court. Vaguely you think of the press tent and the millions of words that will come alive from the busy clucking of the chattering telegraph keys. Where are all those brilliant strokes, the days, the months, the years of practice? It's too quiet. Your nerves are screaming. Your muscles, so perfectly disciplined in practice, seem to have gone in business for themselves. You hear that murmur of expectancy like the wind rustling the leaves on an autumn day. It's the day of a tournament.

For some of you, that will be the big thrill of tennis—tournaments, trophies, ranking, travel, and your name in the newspapers for all to see and admire. Others couldn't care less. I have two competitive sons who eat, live and breathe tennis and who look forward to the first day of each tournament as if it were Christmas. Another athletic son with beautiful strokes, calmly announces, "I'm a social player," and would just as soon miss the tournament and practice his guitar.

Junior tournaments are limited to those under 18 but there are separate divisions for the under 18, under 16, under 14, under 12 and under 10. Some California and Florida tournaments have even scheduled events for the under eight. I was a very backward child since my first tournament experience came at 14. These days, you're a failure if you don't have a room full of trophies by then.

TOURNEY TEMPERAMENT

People often watch a good player in practice and cannot understand why he or she is unable to win the big tournaments. It is hard to see the difference between a good player and a winning one—temperament, experience, nerve, competitive courage, and the confidence which comes from sound stroking ability—all play a part.

It's a long road from practice to actual tournament competition and this is what makes championship tennis a game with which you have to grow up through the years. It is possible to learn the basic strokes in a shorter amount of time, but the knowledge and ability necessary for success in tournament play is something which can be acquired only through many competitive matches.

Some educators have argued that too early competition in any line is bad for a youngster. But others feel that learning to accept victory or defeat helps a boy or girl to mature. It is hard, of course to control your emotions. One young man, now 18 and a model of excellent sportsmanship as a ranking junior in the United States, used to toss his racket (gently?) into the fence. We had a rule at the Edgemoor Club in

Bethesda, Md., that any junior who threw his racket had to go home for the day. I sometimes wonder how he developed into such a fine player with so little practice. I can remember letting go a few rackets myself. My mother promptly cancelled my entry to THREE tournaments and from that time on my racket and I operated as one. Usually by the time the juniors are 15 or 16 the screams and histrionics are down to a minimum.

CONDUCT IN TOURNAMENTS

Children are welcomed at baseball games, especially by the hot dog and peanut vendors. Baseball players are accustomed to playing ball while thousands of vociferous fans scream advice or insult. Tennis players are used to an appreciative knowledgeable gallery which sits in almost dead silence until the point is over. With this background, it is not surprising that many adult club members would prefer that the juniors spend their time in the swimming pool with their vocal chords under water.

There are certain rules to follow—in or out of tournaments. Don't swear and don't throw your racket. If you feel that you must either say something or explode, try "great shot". When you've just lost four points in a row by unforced errors, it may come out rather sarcastically but you can smile at the same time. (You can?) Don't bang the head of the racket on the ground. This may release some of your tensions but it requires an almost unlimited supply of rackets. Hit yourself on the leg or elsewhere which is a self limiting action. When it hurts too much, you'll stop.

Don't fool around on the court. It may seem hysterically funny to you when you and your buddy try to blast each other in the stomach with a tennis ball but it's not going to do a thing for the four men playing a serious match on the next court. When a ball rolls over into your court, wait until a point is not in progress and return it graciously.

Almost all clubs give the senior members preference over the juniors, and justifiably so. Bow off gracefully when your court is preempted and remember that, although it seems absolutely impossible now, you too will be a senior some day.

Seniors also should observe tennis rules and etiquette. When you're playing the increasingly popular winter indoor tennis, remember that sound carries more in a confined place and try to observe the same standards you expect, receive and give in your business.

The great Billie Jean King who, together with World Tennis *publisher Gladys Heldman, has done so much to insure financial success of women's tennis through the Virginia Slims tour.*

SPORTMANSHIP

Give your opponent the benefit of the doubt when calling the lines. I heard of one girl who midway through the second set called her "blind" opponent to the net and told her—"If I were you I'd insist on a referee from now on". When the girl asked why she said "because the way you've been seeing the lines I'm going to start calling OUT when the ball is in the middle of the court". However, it's usually not a good idea to "get even" or the court will get smaller and smaller.

If you're playing in a tournament, always remember to go to the net and shake hands after the match and also thank the referee. You can go over the net if you're sure you won't catch your toe and break a net or a nose.

Arthur Ashe, soft spoken and always the complete gentleman on and off the court.

Ashe returns serve in Davis Cup match.

Don't be discouraged if it takes you a long time to reach anything approaching the top of the ladder. It's a wonderful thing to be striving wholeheartedly towards a goal and it's really much more fun when you are on the way up than when you've finally achieved your ambition. Then everyone will be trying to beat you and it's a mighty precarious perch on that top rung.

I found out how much easier it was to play good tennis when you had everything to win and nothing to lose, while as the champion I was in the position of having to win with not quite the same enthusiasm nor incentive. It's been true of every sport ever since David knocked over Goliath. The Davids are always present to train and work and dream of levelling the Goliaths. It must have been just another match for Goliath when he met David.

TENNIS TRAINING

Training in tennis means following a few simple rules. Do a lot of running to strengthen your legs and jump rope to help with your footwork. Don Brown, an excellent young Michigan professional, has certain exercises with a jump rope with which he keeps his pupils agile and eager. Some of the Professional Lawn Tennis Association (PLTA) professionals are former physical education teachers and virtually all are experts on conditioning. Some of the boys wear weights while running which makes them faster after they're removed. (Sounds like hitting yourself on the head because it feels so good when you stop.)

For Juniors, any athlete knows that avoiding smoking, drinking and marijuana and getting a minimum of eight hours sleep per night will help with speed and endurance. Hot tea is better for you during and after a match than ice cold drinks—(don't like tea!); steak is better than hamburgers (can't afford steak!); order vegetables with your hamburgers rather than french fries (what are vegetables?); take a shower or bath every night or immediately after a tough match. (EVERY night?)

For Seniors, meaning anyone over the advanced age of 35,—Cut down to two packs per day, two martinis before dinner, and don't practice TOO much or you might end up with tennis elbow or back strain.

If you occasionally get cramps on a hot day, take two salt tablets with two glasses of water several hours before starting play. If you have blisters on hands or feet, bandaids may not stick. Apply moleskin well ahead of time. As a preventive measure, tincture of benzoin is useful. Or take out insurance with an S. A. I glove.

Don't eat too much just because the food is free. My first experience of being "put up" as a junior tennis player was a one week tournament held at the Coronado Beach Hotel in Southern California. I was so carried away by the idea of signing for meals that I ate myself out of the tournament in an early round.

There was a much later tournament at the Westchester Country Club in Rye, New York where the Eastern Grass Court Championships were held. (They've since been moved to Orange, N.J.) The committee put up only a few players but Doris Hart and I were allotted a room and meals. Since our many friends among the players had little money, we added a few cots, utilized the soft floor, and seven of us made it through the week. Doris and I ordered two large breakfasts with seven forks and Mary Arnold Prentiss always travelled with a large jar of peanut butter which took care of lunch. Ed Sullivan was living at the club and, although a golfer, usually felt sorry for the poor travelling tennis players and provided a few dinners. Before he became a syndicated columnist and prominent television personality, Ed had started as a sports writer and was responsible for Helen Wills' famous nickname of "Little Miss Poker Face."

100

Bob Lutz, national pro champion in 1972.

Chris Evert and Evonne Goolagong are both victims of the feud between the Virginia Slims group and the USLTA and currently will play only USLTA-sanctioned matches.

Australian Yvonne Goolagong, former Wimbledon champion.

Harold Solomon, who played in Davis Cup matches against Spain in 1972 in spite of being threatened by terrorists.

Rosemary Casals, San Francisco, California, second leading money winner on the Virginia Slims professional tour.

TYPES OF COURTS

Travelling to tournaments means that you must become accustomed to playing on various types of surfaces. While there has long been a cry for a uniform playing surface throughout the world, varying climatic conditions and difficulties of upkeep, plus tradition, govern the type of court in a particular location. English followers of the game know well the grass courts of Queens and Wimbledon. But in the States, many a Texan believes that the Forest Hills tournaments (the National Championships) are played on a hard sun-baked clay. (They're played on grass.) Some Californians assume that cement or asphalt is the only known surface for court construction. It's difficult to imagine anything other than your own experience, which is the reason many Eastern club members are incredulous that tennis should be played on cement.

The dwindling supply of caretakers gradually has decreased the number of courts which require upkeep and has, through necessity, brought about radical composition changes.

Emulsions of asphalt and cork, or asphalt and rubber, are replacing the pampered clay courts at various clubs. These courts, called Grasstex or Cork Carpet or Satinturf or Dynaturf, have the playing characteristics of clay in that they give a relatively slow bounce. But they need only to be swept or vacuum-cleaned rather than extensively dragged, watered and rolled. Plain cement or asphalt is cheaper but is a much faster surface and harder on the feet.

The new indoor facilities are bypassing clay and Har-Tru in favor of some form of composition such as Satinturf or an actual carpet such as Sportface or the Swedish Bolltex. Especially on those courts covered by an inflated air bubble, the humidity problem is increased if a surface is used which requires constant watering.

Grass, too, with its disappearing baselines and many bad bounces, is being phased out. Longwood, Mass., scene of the National Professional Tournament, already has gone to a slow synthetic, Uniturf, and Forest Hills is soon to follow.

The slow courts tend to favor the steady backcourt player who can run down the big shots. The volleyer has a difficult time since some of the sting is taken off a hard hit approach and the high, slower bounce of the ball gives the backcourt player ample time to get set for a passing shot.

Wood, cement and grass, all give an advantage to the hard hitter and the man with the good serve and volley. A twist serve is especially effective since the grass will take the spin. A drop shot is excellent on grass, good on clay, and makes you a candidate for the asylum if you use it on wood.

106

Off Guantanamo, Cuba, when Dorothy "Dodo" Bundy and I were on a U.S.O. tour, we played on the steel hangar deck of the aircraft carrier, U.S.S. Mission Bay. Not only was the surface extremely fast but every time you went back for a lob, you bumped into a sailor or an airplane.

Changing surfaces is difficult and yet I saw those wonderful Aussie professionals, Lew Hoad and Ken Rosewall, play on clay one afternoon and the next night move into Tokyo and bring 7000 screaming fans to their feet with their brilliant shots off a slick wood floor.

Chris Evert is one of tennis' bright new stars. Her father is Ft. Lauderdale teaching pro Jim Evert, a high ranking amateur in the 1940's.

CHAPTER VIII

Conclusion

There is an Irish phrase which hopes that the wind will always be at your back. Tennis has many headwinds, but, generally, it will be at your back when you pick up that racket and start to learn.

Be a social player or a competitor—it does not matter. The game is there for you, whether you want it for fun or for a lifetime of tournaments and travel.

But enjoyment of the world of tennis is not only for the champions. Tennis can mean health and pride in accomplishment, large or small. It can be a game to brush away the cobwebs after long study. It can take the edge off boredom and fill each hour with fun and excitement. Tennis can mean many friendships and the opening up of a whole new world. Once you get over the "boot camp" or basic training of tennis, you will know that somebody really unlocked the doors to something wonderful.

The end of the rainbow, Rod Laver holds the Champion's Cup at Wimbledon.

OFFICIAL
LAWN TENNIS RULES

as issued by
UNITED STATES
LAWN TENNIS ASSOCIATION

RULES OF LAWN TENNIS

EXPLANATORY NOTE

The appended Code of Rules is the Official Code of the International Lawn Tennis Federation, of which the United States Lawn Tennis Association is a member.

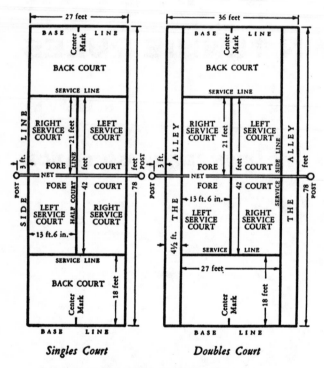

Singles Court   *Doubles Court*

DIAGRAM AND DIMENSIONS OF
TENNIS COURT

THE SINGLES GAME

RULE 1: DIMENSIONS AND EQUIPMENT

The Court shall be a rectangle, 78 feet long and 27 feet wide. It shall be divided across the middle by a net, suspended from a cord or metal cable of a maximum diameter of one-third of an inch, the ends of which shall be attached to, or pass over, the tops of two posts, 3 feet, 6 inches high, the center of which shall stand 3 feet outside the Court on each side. The height of the net shall be 3 feet at the center, where it shall be held down taut by a strap not more than 2 inches wide. There shall be a band covering the cord or metal cable and the top of the net for not less than 2 inches nor more than 2 1/2 inches in depth on each side. The lines bounding the ends and sides of the Court shall respectively be called the Base-lines and the Side-lines. On each side of the net, at a distance of 21 feet from it and parallel with it, shall be drawn the Service-lines. The space on each side of the net between the Service-line and the Side-lines shall be divided into two equal parts called the Service-Courts by the center Service-line, which must be 2 inches in width, drawn half-way between, and parallel with, the Side-lines. Each Base-line shall be bisected by an imaginary continuation of the center Service-line to a line 4 inches in length and 2 inches in width called the center mark drawn inside the Court, at right angles to and in contact with such Base-lines. All other lines shall be not less than 1 inch nor more than 2 inches in width, except the Base-line, which may be 4 inches in width, and all measurements shall be made to the outside of the lines.

Note.—In the case of the International Lawn Tennis Championship (Davis Cup) or other Official Championships of the International Federation, there shall be a space behind each Base-line of not less than 21 feet, and at the sides of not less than 12 feet.

RULE 2: PERMANENT FIXTURES

The permanent fixtures of the Court shall include not only the net, posts, cord or metal cable, strap and band, but also, where there are any such, the back and side stops, the stands, fixed or movable seats and chairs round the Court, and their occupants, all other fixtures around and above the Court, and the Umpire, Footfault Judge and Linesmen when in their respective places.

Note.—For the purpose of Rule 2, the word "Umpire" comprehends the umpire and all those persons designated to assist him in the conduct of a match.

RULE 3: BALL—SIZE, WEIGHT AND BOUND

The ball shall have a uniform outer surface. If there are any seams they shall be stitchless. The ball shall be more than two and a half inches and less than two and five-eights inches in diameter, and more than two ounces and less than two and one-sixteenth ounces in weight. The ball shall have a bound of more than 53 inches and less than 58 inches when dropped 100 inches upon a concrete base, and a deformation of more than .265 of an inch and less than .290 of an inch when subjected to a pressure of 18 lb. applied to each end of any diameter.

RULE 4: SERVER AND RECEIVER

The players shall stand on opposite sides of the net; the player who first delivers the ball shall be called the Server, and the other the Receiver.

RULE 5: CHOICE OF SIDES AND SERVICE

The choice of sides, and the right to be Server or Receiver in the first game shall be decided by toss. The player winning the toss may choose or require his opponent to choose:

(a) The right to be Server or Receiver, in which case the other player shall choose the side; or

(b) The side, in which case the other player shall choose the right to be Server or Receiver.

RULE 6: DELIVERY OF SERVICE

The service shall be delivered in the following manner: Immediately before commencing to serve, the Server shall stand with both feet at rest behind (i.e. farther from the net than) the base-line, and within the imaginary continuations of the center-mark and side-line. The Server shall then project the ball by hand into the air in any direction and before it hits the ground strike it with his racket, and the delivery shall be deemed to have been completed at the moment of the impact of the racket and the ball. A player with the use of only one arm may utilize his racket for the projection.

RULE 7: FOOT FAULT

The Server shall throughout the delivery of the service:

(a) Not change his position by walking or running.

(b) Not touch with either foot, any area other than that behind the base-line within the imaginary extension of the center mark and side-line.

The revised rule permits a player to swing his foot over the base-line in serving provided he does not touch the surface of the court inside the base-line before he strikes the ball. It also permits the player to jump off the ground when serving.

RULE 8: FROM ALTERNATE COURTS

(a) In delivering the service, the Server shall stand alternately behind the right and left Courts, beginning from the right in every game. If service from a wrong half of the Court occurs and is undetected, all play resulting from such wrong service or services shall stand, but the inaccuracy of the station shall be corrected immediately it is discovered.

(b) The ball served shall pass over the net and hit the ground within the Service Court which is diagonally opposite, or upon any line bounding such Court, before the Receiver returns it.

RULE 9: FAULTS

The Service is a fault:

(a) If the Server commit any breach of Rules 6, 7 or 8;

(b) If he miss the ball in attempting to strike it;

(c) If the ball served touch a permanent fixture (other than the net, strap or band) before it hits the ground.

RULE 10: SERVICE AFTER A FAULT

After a fault (if it be the first fault) the Server shall serve again from behind the same half of the Court from which he served that fault, unless the service was from the wrong half, when, in accordance with Rule 8, the Server shall be entitled to one service only from behind the other half. A fault may not be claimed after the next service has been delivered.

RULE 11: RECEIVER MUST BE READY

The Server shall not serve until the Receiver is ready. If the latter attempt to return the service, he shall be deemed ready. If, however, the Receiver signify that he is not ready, he may not claim a fault because the ball does not hit the ground within the limits fixed for the service.

RULE 12: A LET

In all cases where a Let has to be called under the rules, or to provide for an interruption to play, it shall have the following interpretation:
  (a) When called solely in respect of a service, that one service only shall be replayed.
  (b) When called under any other circumstance, the point shall be replayed.

RULE 13: THE SERVICE IS A LET

  (a) If the ball served touch the net, strap or band, and is otherwise good, or, after touching the net, strap or band, touch the Receiver or anything which he wears or carries before hitting the ground.
  (b) If a service or a fault be delivered when the Receiver is not ready (see Rule 11). In case of a Let, that particular service shall not count, and the Server shall serve again, but a Service does not annul a previous fault.

RULE 14: WHEN RECEIVER BECOMES SERVER

At the end of the first game the Receiver shall become Server, and the Server, Receiver; and so on alternately in all the subsequent games of a match. If a player serve out of turn, the player who ought to have served shall serve as soon as the mistake is discovered, but all points scored before such discovery shall be reckoned. If a game shall have been completed before such discovery, the order of service remains as altered. A fault served before such discovery shall not be reckoned.

RULE 15: BALL IN PLAY TILL POINT DECIDED

A ball is in play from the moment at which it is delivered in service. Unless a fault or a let be called, it remains in play until the point is decided.

RULE 16: SERVER WINS POINT

The Server wins the point:
  (a) If the ball served, not being a let under Rule 13, touch the Receiver or anything which he wears or carries, before it hits the ground.
  (b) If the Receiver otherwise lose the point as provided by Rule 18.

RULE 17: RECEIVER WINS POINT

The Receiver wins the point:
  (a) If the Server serve two consecutive faults;
  (b) If the Server otherwise lose the point as provided by Rule 18.

RULE 18: PLAYER LOSES POINT

A player loses the point if:
  (a) He fail, before the ball in play has hit the ground twice consecutively, to return it directly over the net (except as provided in Rule 22 (a) or (c); or
  (b) He return the ball in play so that it hits the ground, a permanent fixture, or other object, outside any of the lines which bound his opponent's Court (except as provided in Rule 22 (a) and (c); or
  (c) He volley the ball and fail to make a good return even when standing outside the Court; or
  (d) He touch or strike the ball in play with his racket more than once in making a stroke; or
  (e) He or his racket (in his hand or otherwise) or anything which he wears or carries touch the net, posts, cord or metal cable, strap or band, or the ground within his opponent's Court at any time while the ball is in play; or
  (f) He volley the ball before it has passed the net; or

(g) The ball in play touch him or anything that he wears or carries, except his racket in his hand or hands; or

(h) He throws his racket at and hits the ball.

RULE 19: PLAYER HINDERS OPPONENT

If a player commits any act either deliberate or involuntary which, in the opinion of the Umpire, hinders his opponent in making a stroke, the Umpire shall in the first case award the point to the opponent, and in the second case order the point to be replayed.

RULE 20: BALL FALLING ON LINE—GOOD

A ball falling on a line is regarded as falling in the Court bounded by that line.

RULE 21: BALL TOUCHING PERMANENT FIXTURE

If the ball in play touch a permanent fixture (other than the net, posts, cord or metal cable, strap or band) after it has hit the ground, the player who struck it wins the point; if before it hits the ground his opponent wins the point.

RULE 22: GOOD RETURN

It is a good return:

(a) If the ball touch the net, posts, cord or metal cable, strap or band, provided that it passes over any of them and hits the ground within the Court; or

(b) If the ball, served or returned, hit the ground within the proper Court and rebound or be blown back over the net, and the player whose turn it is to strike reach over the net and play the ball, provided that neither he nor any part of his clothes or racket touch the net, posts, cord or metal cable, strap or band or the ground within his opponent's Court, and that the stroke be otherwise good; or

(c) If the ball be returned outside the post, either above or below the level of the top of the net, even though it touch the post, provided that it hits the ground within the proper Court; or

(d) If a player's racket pass over the net after he has returned the ball, provided the ball pass the net before being played and be properly returned; or

(e) If a player succeeded in returning the ball, served or in play, which strikes a ball lying in the Court.

RULE 23: INTERFERENCE

In case a player is hindered in making a stroke by anything not within his control except a permanent fixture of the Court, or except as provided for in Rule 19, the point shall be replayed.

RULE 24: THE GAME

If a player wins his first point, the score is called *15* for that player; on winning his second point, the score is called *30* for that player; on winning his third point, the score is called *40* for that player, and the fourth point won by a player is scored *game* for that player except as below:

If both players have won three points, the score is called *deuce;* and the next point won by a player is called *advantage* for that player. If the same player wins the next point, he wins the game; if the other player wins the next point the score is again called *deuce;* and so on, until a player wins the two points immediately following the score at deuce, when the game is scored for that player.

RULE 25: THE SET

A player (or players) who first wins six games wins a set; except that he must win by a margin of at least two games over his opponent and where necessary a set shall be extended until this margin be achieved.

RULE 26: WHEN PLAYERS CHANGE SIDES

The players shall change sides at the end of the first, third and every sub-sequent alternate game of each set, and at the end of each set unless the total number of games in such set be even, in which case the change is not made until the end of the first game of the next set.

RULE 27: MAXIMUM NUMBER OF SETS

The maximum number of sets in a match shall be 5, or, where women take part, 3.

RULE 28: RULES APPLY TO BOTH SEXES

Except where otherwise stated, every reference in these Rules to the masculine includes the feminine gender.

RULE 29: DECISIONS OF UMPIRE AND REFEREE

In matches where an Umpire is appointed, his decision shall be final; but where a Referee is appointed, an appeal shall lie to him from the decision of an Umpire on a question of law, and in all such cases the decision of the Referee shall be final.

The Referee, in his discretion, may at any time postpone a match on account of darkness or the condition of the ground or the weather. In any case of post-ponement the previous score and previous occupancy of Courts shall hold good, unless the Referee and the players unanimously agree otherwise.

RULE 30:

Play shall be continuous from the first service till the match be concluded; provided that after the third set, or when women take part, the second set, either player is entitled to a rest, which shall not exceed 10 minutes, or in countries situated between Latitude 15 degrees North and Latitude 15 degrees South, 45 minutes, and provided further that when necessitated by circumstances not within the control of the players, the Umpire may suspend play for such a period as he may consider necessary. If play be suspended and be not resumed until a later day the rest may be taken only after the third set (or when women take part the second set) of play on such later day, completion of an unfinished set being counted as one set. These provisions shall be strictly construed, and play shall never be suspended, delayed or interfered with for the purpose of enabling a player to recover his strength or his wind, or to receive instruction or advice. The Umpire shall be the sole judge of such suspension, delay or interference, and after giving due warning he may disqualify the offender.

THE DOUBLES GAME

RULE 31:

The foregoing Rules shall apply to the Doubles Game except as below.

RULE 32: DIMENSIONS OF COURT

For the Doubles Game, the Court shall be 36 feet in width, i.e. 4 1/2 feet wider on each side than the Court for the Singles Game, and those portions of the singles side-lines which lie between the two service-lines shall be called the service-side-lines. In other respects, the Court shall be similar to that described in Rule 1, but the portions of the singles side-lines between the base-line and service-line on each side of the net may be omitted if desired.

RULE 33: ORDER OF SERVICE

The order of serving shall be decided at the beginning of each set as follows:

The pair who have to serve in the first game of each set shall decide which partner shall do so and the opposing pair shall decide similarly for the second game. The partner of the player who served in the first game shall serve in the third; the partner of the player who served in the second game shall serve in the fourth, and so on in the same order in all the subsequent games of a set.

RULE 34: ORDER OF RECEIVING

The order of receiving the service shall be decided at the beginning of each set as follows:

The pair who have to receive the service in the first game shall decide which partner shall receive the first service, and that partner shall continue to receive the first service in every odd game throughout that set. The opposing pair shall likewise decide which partner shall receive the first service in the second game and that partner shall continue to receive the first service in every even game throughout that set. Partners shall receive the service alternately throughout each game.

RULE 35: SERVICE OUT OF TURN

If a partner serve out of his turn, the partner who ought to have served shall serve as soon as the mistake is discovered, but all points scored, and any faults served before such discovery, shall be reckoned. If a game shall have been completed before such discovery, the order of service remains as altered.

RULE 36: ERROR IN ORDER OF RECEIVING

If during a game the order of receiving the service is changed by the receivers it shall remain as altered until the end of the game in which the mistake is discovered, but the partners shall resume their original order of receiving in the next game of that set in which they are receivers of the service.

RULE 37: BALL TOUCHING SERVERS PARTNER IS FAULT

The service is a fault as provided for by Rule 9, or if the ball served touch the Server's partner or anything he wears or carries, but if the ball served touch the partner of the Receiver or anything which he wears or carries, not being a let under Rule 13 (a), before it hits the ground, the Server wins the point.

RULE 38: BALL STRUCK ALTERNATELY

The ball shall be struck alternately by one or other player of the opposing pairs, and if a player touches the ball in play with his racket in contravention of this Rule, his opponents win the point.

WHAT TO DO WHEN THE SCORE REACHES 6-6.......

Singles: If it is Player A's turn to serve the 13th game (at 6-all), he shall serve Points 1 and 2, right court and left court; Player B then serves Points 3 and 4 (R and L). Players then change sides, and A serves Point 5 and 6; B serves Points 7 and 8. If the score reaches 4 points-all, Player B serves Point 9 from the right or left court at the election of the receiver.

The set shall be recorded as 7 games to 6. The tie-break counts as one game in reckoning ball-changes.

Player B shall serve first in the set following the playing of the tie-break (thus assuring that he will be first server if this set also goes into a tie-break). The players shall "stay for one" after a tie-break.

118

If both the first two sets in a best-of-three set match or if either two or four sets in a best-of-five set match end in tie-break games, the players shall spin a racket at the start of the final set to establish service order and side. (Umpires should note that, if this results in a change in serving sequence, the next ball change, if any, should be deferred one game to preserve the alternation of the right to serve first with new balls.)

Doubles: In doubles the same format as in singles applies, provided that each player shall serve from the same end of the court in the tie-break game that he has served from during that particular set. (The tie-break sequence shall count as one game for ball-change reckoning.)

Singles: Player A shall serve Points 1 and 2, right court and left court; Player B serves Points 3 and 4; A serves Points 5 and 6. The players then change sides; B serves Points 7 and 8; A serves Points 9 and 10; B serves Points 11 and 12. If either player wins 7 points, the set is recorded 7 games to 6. If the score of the tie-break game reaches 6 points-all, the players shall change sides and play shall continue with serve alternating on every point until one player establishes a margin of 2 points, as follows:

A serves the 13th point (right court), B serves Point 14 (right); A serves Point 15 (left); B serves Point 16 (left). If the score is still tied, the players change sides every 4 points and repeat this procedure.

Player B shall serve first in the set following the playing of the tie-break. The players shall "stay for one."

If both the first two sets in a best-of-three-set match or if either two or four sets in a best-of-five-set match end in tie-break games, the players shall spin a racket at the start of the final set to establish service order and side.

Doubles (A and B v. C and D): Assuming that Player D has served the 12th game to make the score 6 games-all, the teams shall "stay" for the first 2 points of the tie-break, then change sides and change every 4 points thereafter during the first 12 points. A shall serve Points 1 and 2, right court and left court; change sides; C serves Points 3 and 4; B serves Points 5 and 6; change sides; D serves Points 7 and 8; A serves Points 9 and 10; change sides; C serves Points 11 and 12. If either team wins 7 points, the set is recorded 7 games to 6.

If the score of the tie-break game reaches 6 points-all, B shall serve Point 13 from the right court; change sides; D serves Point 14 from the right court; A serves Point 15 from the left court; change sides; C serves Point 16 from the left court; B serves Point 17 from the right court; change sides and so on.

Upon completion of the tie-break game, the teams shall "stay for one", and either C or D (members of the team who served the last full game before the tie-break) shall serve the first game of the next set.

If both the first two sets in a best-of-three-set match, or if either two or four sets in a best-of-five-set match, end in tie-break games, the players shall spin a racket at the start of the final set to establish service order and side.

The tie-break counts as one game in reckoning ball changes.

Note: Should any point arise upon which you find it difficult to give a decision or on which you are in doubt as to the proper ruling, immediately write, giving full details to the Tennis Umpires Association, care of USLTA, 120 Broadway, New York 5, N. Y., and full instructions and explanations will be sent you.

THE AMERICAN FILM HERITAGE
Impressions from The American Film Institute Archives
Foreword by Gregory Peck

America has had a love affair with the movies for a long seventy-five year run! THE AMERICAN FILM HERITAGE shows why. From silents to shorts, to animation, to the advent of color and sound, the Warner Musicals, the "B" Western, the Black film experience—and much more. A splendid series of impressions selected by AFI brings to life a wide range of your favorite movies, actors, directors, etc. Film experts such as Stephen F. Zito, William K. Everson, and Tom Shales have written 34 articles to help you recapture the early days of American film, this century's foremost art form.

"Films also have significance as historical and sociological documents. They retain the power not only to delight us, but to enlighten us as well. As art and as history, they are being secured and preserved as a valuable part of our cultural heritage."—GREGORY PECK, from the Foreword

"A shattering artistic and emotional experience could be in store for readers of this collection of impressions of the American Film Institute. . . . filled with nostalgic sidebars about the infant years of the American film industry . . . accounts of successful film rescue missions of the AFI"— *Smithsonian Magazine*

"In this volume the American Film Institute takes on the outlines of a brave strong ship, moving in full scholarly and dedicated sail, back into yesterday's storm tossed waters, with the artistic mission of rescuing lost movies. . . . A whole variety of impressions are packed into the thirty-four chapters." —*Hollywood Reporter*

"Film buffs will have a ball leafing through these pages with their unfamiliar stills from long-forgotten movies. The book is heavily illustrated and the text, by well-known film personalities, is replete with entertaining and enlightening film talk."— John Barkham, *Saturday Review Syndicate*

$17.50 deluxe hardbound with handsome silver sleeve box
$4.95 paperback

THE "NOW" LIBRARY
A Station Approach Media Center Teaching Kit
By Mary Margrabe   **$6.50** paper
Not just for librarians **but for anyone interested in developing media service skills. A basic resource guide to teaching within a media center. Includes teaching kit.**

THE ELEMENTS OF EFFECTIVE COMMUNICATION
Idea Power Tactics   **$6.50** cloth
By W. A. Mambert   **$3.95** paper
What Strunk and White's ELEMENTS OF STYLE did for writing, this book will do for human communication.
". . . Offers much practical advice for the student or professional wanting to communicate more effectively."—*The Quill*